What Makes a Community?

Janet Helenthal

PICTURE CREDITS

Cover, page 34-b © Michael S. Yamashita/Corbis; title page (left & right), pages 9 (bottom right), 11 (left), 35-d © Getty Images; title page (center) © Creatas/ PictureQuest; pages 2-3 © Cathy Melloan/PhotoEdit; pages 5 (top left), 7 (inset right), 9 (top right), 9 (bottom left), 10 (bottom right), 16 (flag), 25 (top left), 31 (bottom) © Corbis; page 5 (bottom left) © Bob Rowan/Corbis; page 5 (right) © Alamy Images; pages 6-7, 25 (top right) © Elizabeth Hathon/Corbis; pages 7-11 (backgrounds) © David Young-Wolff/PhotoEdit; page 7 (left inset) © Owaki-Kulla/Corbis; page 8 (top), 35-f © Don Mason/Corbis; pages 8 (bottom), 34-a © Erik Freeland/Corbis; pages 9 (top left), 10 (top right), 26 (bottom), 34-e © David R. Frazier; pages 10 (top left), 25 (bottom left), 35-c © Henry Diltz/Corbis; page 10 (bottom left) © Bill Stormont/Corbis; page 11 (right) © Patrick Bennett/Corbis; pages 12, 25 (bottom right), 34-f © Nancy Richmond/The Image Works; page 13 (top left) © Ellen Sirisi/The Image Works; pages 13 (top right), 35-b © Sonda Dawes/The Image Works; page 13 (bottom left) © Alan Schein Photography/Corbis; page 13 (bottom right) © Joe Sohm/Alamy; page 14 © Chuck Savage/Corbis; page 15 © Paul Barton/Corbis; pages 16-17 © Robert Brenner/PhotoEdit Inc.; page 17 (inset) illustration by Rose Zgodzinski; pages 18, 19 (right), 35-a © Bettmann/Corbis; page 19 (left) Library of Congress; pages 20 (top), 34-c © Jonathan Blair/Corbis; page 20 (bottom) © Brown Brothers; pages 21, 23, 34-d © Bob Krist/Corbis; page 22 © Catherine Karnow/Corbis; page 26 (top) © Ed Young/Corbis; page 27 (top and bottom) © Ann Hawthorne/Corbis; page 28 © Jim Olive/Peter Arnold, Inc.; page 29 © Jeff Greenberg/Danita Delimont Stock Photography; page 30 (top left) © Syracuse Newspapers/David Lassman/The Image Works; page 30 (top right) © Roy Morsch/Corbis; page 31 (top) © Joel Stettenheim/ Corbis, (center) © Paul Barton/Corbis; page 32 © David Hiller/Getty Images; page 33 (left) *Communities Across America Today* by Sarah Glasscock, © 2002 National Geographic Society, illustration © 1993 Carmen Lomas Garza, photo © M. Lee Fatherree; page 33 (center) *Caracas, Venezuela* by Elspeth Leacock, © 2003 National Geographic Society, photo © Pable Corral V/Corbis, (inset) © Ulrike Welsch; page 33 (right) *A Suburban Community of the 1950s* by Gare Thompson, © 2002 National Geographic Society, photo © Wood River Gallery/PictureQuest; page 36 © Spencer Grant/PhotoEdit.

Produced through the worldwide resources of the National Geographic Society, John M. Fahey Jr., President and Chief Executive Officer; Gilbert M. Grosvenor, Chairman of the Board; Nina D. Hoffman, Executive Vice President and President, Books and Education Publishing Group.

PREPARED BY NATIONAL GEOGRAPHIC SCHOOL PUBLISHING

Ericka Markman, Senior Vice President and President, Children's Books and Education Publishing Group; Steve Mico, Senior Vice President, Editorial Director, Publisher; Francis Downey, Executive Editor; Richard Easby, Editorial Manager; Anne Stone, Lori Dibble Collins, Editors; Bea Jackson, Director of Layout and Design; Jim Hiscott, Design Manager; Cynthia Olson, Art Director; Margaret Sidlosky, Illustrations Director; Matt Wascavcge, Manager of Publishing Services; Sean Philpotts, Jane Ponton, Production Managers; Ted Tucker, Production Specialist.

MANUFACTURING AND QUALITY CONTROL

Christopher A. Liedel, Chief Financial Officer; Phillip L. Schlosser, Director; Clifton M. Brown III, Manager

◀ School kids paint a mural in their community.

Contents

CONSULTANT AND REVIEWER
Sam Goldberger, professor emeritus, Capital Community College,
Hartford, Connecticut

BOOK DESIGN/PHOTO RESEARCH
Steve Curtis Design, Inc.

Published by the National Geographic Society
1145 17th Street N.W.
Washington, D.C. 20036-4688

ISBN: 0-7922-5454-6
ISBN-13: 978-0-7922-5454-6

2012
     4 5 6 7 8 9 10 11 12 13 14 15

Printed in Canada.

What Is a Com

Think about where you live. Do other people live close by? Are there stores and parks? Are there schools?

You live in a **community.** A community is a place where people live, work, and have fun together. All communities have some things in common.

Look at these pictures. They show things that most communities have. What else can you find in a community? In this book, you will learn what a community is and does.

....

community – a place where people live, work, and have fun together

▲ **A place to play**

▲ **A place to shop**

munity?

▲ A place to live

▲ A place to work

Big Idea
Communities meet people's needs.

Set Purpose
Read to learn how communities meet people's needs.

Questions You Will Explore

Why do people live in communities?

How do communities meet people's needs?

Communities
Meet People's Needs

People live in communities. Communities have things that people want and need. Communities have houses, stores, and jobs. They also keep people safe and comfortable. Communities meet people's needs.

Communities Have Housing

People need places to live. Communities have houses and **apartments** where people can live. These homes give people **shelter** from the weather. They **provide** people with places to keep their things.

....

apartment – a group of rooms where people live

shelter – protection

provide – to give or supply

▲ Houses are also part of a community.

▼ Some people live in buildings with many apartments.

Communities Have Stores

People need food, clothes, and other **goods.**
Communities have stores and markets that sell
goods. People buy the goods they need at stores
in the community.

....

goods – things that are made or grown and then sold

Goods

food

clothes

tools

books

Communities Have Services

People need **services.** A service is something useful that one person does for another. Communities provide many kinds of services. Police and firefighters protect people. Trash collectors pick up garbage. Postal carriers deliver mail. Teachers teach.

....

service – something useful that one person does for another

Services

mail delivery

garbage collection

emergency services

education

Communities Have Transportation

Transportation is another service communities provide. People need ways to get from place to place. They need to get to work or school.

Communities build and fix roads for people to drive on. Some communities have **public transportation.** They have buses and subways for people to ride on.

....

public transportation – a way of moving large numbers of people from place to place

▲ **A bus is one kind of public transportation.**

Communities Have Governments

People need the services in their communities to run smoothly. So they elect officials to form **governments.** A government is the group of people who run a community.

Communities need money to pay for the services they provide. Governments collect taxes from the people who live and work there. Taxes pay for the services communities provide.

....

government – a group of people who run a community

▲ **People talk about community problems at a town meeting.**

Communities Have Rules

People need to get along with each other. Communities make rules that everyone agrees to follow. The rules tell people how to behave.

Community rules are called **laws.** Laws help keep people safe. They help people get along with one another. Signs can help us remember rules. For example, signs tell us where we can ride our bikes.

....

law – a community rule

Signs

stop sign

no bicycles

no parking

no littering

13

Communities Have Jobs

People need money to pay for goods and services. To earn money, they need to work. Communities provide jobs for people. They help people find work.

▼ **Local stores provide work for people.**

Communities Have Places to Play

People need places to have fun. Many communities have parks and playgrounds. People can play ball and hike in the parks. People can see concerts in the parks.

People look for places to play when they choose a place to live. People also look for good jobs, schools, places to shop, and lots of other services.

Stop and Think!

HOW do communities meet people's needs?

▲ A family enjoys a picnic in a park.

Recap
Describe ways that communities meet people's needs.

Set Purpose
Read about a famous community in New York City.

Little

▲ People walk in the streets of Little Italy.

Italy

Little Italy is a small community in a big city. It is only a few blocks wide. People live and work in Little Italy. They eat at the restaurants and food stands. They shop for things they need. Little Italy is one of New York City's many communities.

Little Italy

New York City

Manhattan

Brooklyn

Immigrants Arrive in New York

Immigrants are people who move from one country to another. They leave their homeland and settle in a new country. From about 1880 to 1920, millions of immigrants came to the United States. They came from around the world.

Many new immigrants moved to New York City. The city was filled with people who had different **customs** from their own. New Yorkers spoke many different languages. They ate different foods. It was all so new and strange!

immigrant – a person who leaves home to settle in a new country
custom – a habit or typical way of doing something

▲ **Immigrants wait on Ellis Island in New York Harbor.**

A Place Like Home

In New York City, many immigrants came from Italy. They moved to an area near Mulberry Street. Lots of people from Italy already lived on Mulberry Street. The new immigrants could find jobs there. The food people ate there was just like back in Italy. And people on Mulberry Street spoke Italian. It felt like home.

▲ Italian immigrants shop for food along Mulberry Street.

Little Italy Gets Its Name

So many Italians moved to Mulberry Street that the community was given a new name. It was called "Little Italy."

People lived in tiny apartments. Sometimes parents, children, and grandparents all lived together in one apartment. Aunts and uncles often lived in the same building.

▲ Family members share a traditional Italian meal.

▼ An Italian family crowds into a tiny apartment.

Meeting People's Needs

The people in Little Italy helped newcomers get used to a new country. For example, they helped each other find jobs. They also held Italian **festivals.** They remembered life in Italy.

People in Little Italy had fun playing Italian games such as boccie ball. They grew Italian plants such as basil. They cooked and ate Italian foods such as pizza. They put statues of Italian heroes in the parks. It was like a little part of Italy.

....

festival – a big celebration

▼ Even today, people in Little Italy like to play boccie ball.

Little Italy Today

Today, fewer Italian immigrants are moving to Little Italy. The community has begun to change. Yet Mulberry Street is still the center of the community. And parts of Little Italy are like it was in the past.

Many people there still speak Italian. The smells of tomato sauce and sausage still fill the air. Shops still sell Italian clothing, shoes, statues, and other goods. These things might never change.

▲ The smells from this shop fill the air in Little Italy.

Community Celebration

Every September, the people of Little Italy hold a festival. It is the Feast of San Gennaro. The festival honors the Italian hero San Gennaro. People celebrate for ten days. They come from all around the city. People dance, sing, and eat all day. They play games under the twinkling lights at night. People celebrate Little Italy. They celebrate the community in the past and present.

Stop and Think!

HOW does Little Italy meet people's needs?

▲ **The Feast of San Gennaro**

Recap
Describe how people in Little Italy live, work, and have fun together.

Set Purpose
Read to learn more about people and their communities.

CONNECT WHAT YOU HAVE LEARNED

What Makes a Community?

A community is a place where people live, work, and have fun together. Communities have things that people want and need.

Here are some ideas that you learned about communities.

- Communities give people housing, jobs, and places to play.
- Communities have stores and markets where people can buy goods.
- Communities provide many services to keep people safe and comfortable.
- Communities have governments to help services run smoothly.

Check What You Have Learned

HOW do communities meet people's needs?

▲ Communities give people housing.

▲ Communities have stores and markets.

▲ Communities provide many services.

▲ Communities have governments.

Trade Connects Communities

▲ **Tomatoes are harvested on a farm.**

Communities depend on one another for help meeting people's needs. What happens if you live in a place where tomatoes do not grow well? How do you get tomatoes to eat?

People in different communities sell goods to one another. They use transportation to carry the goods from place to place. A farmer grows tomatoes. Then a truck or train carries them to a market in another state. Now people in that state can buy tomatoes.

Trade connects communities. It is all part of how communities meet people's needs.

◀ McMurdo Station, near the South Pole, is one of the world's coldest communities.

A Community Near the
South Pole

The South Pole is the coldest place on Earth. Temperatures fall far below zero. In the winter, the sun never rises. In the summer, the sun never sets.

Scientists from around the world have set up research stations near the South Pole. One of these is called McMurdo Station. Scientists live there. Their job is to study the land, weather, and sea. McMurdo is one of the world's coldest communities.

▲ Scientists get ready for work near McMurdo.

27

▲ Students connect to an e-community with their computer.

E-communities

Not all communities are in towns and cities. Some are connected by technology. One community is called an "e-community." It is short for "electronic community." Anyone with a computer can join. People in e-communities have fun together. Students, families, and scientists use their computers to talk and share ideas. They meet on the Internet. The Internet links more than 700 million people around the world!

Kids and Communities

Kids help communities in many ways. They can help to make parks, schools, and other places more valuable to the community. What do they do? Some kids plant trees or pick up trash. Others paint murals in community centers and schools. What can you do to help make your community a great place to be?

▶ **These girls are painting a mural.**

Many kinds of words are used in this book. Here you will learn about words that show action. You will also learn about words that have suffixes.

Verbs

A verb is a word that shows action. Find the verbs below. Use each verb in your own sentence.

People usually **work** at jobs in or near their community.

Children **play** basketball on the school playground.

Sometimes people **bike** along trails in their community.

It is fun to **eat** at picnic tables in the park.

Suffixes

A suffix is a group of letters added to the end of a word. A suffix changes the meaning of the word. For example, the suffix *–er* can turn an action into a person, place, or thing.

work + er = worker

A road construction **worker** helps build and fix roads in the community.

play + er = player

A baseball **player** plays with her friends in the park.

farm + er = farmer

A **farmer** works on a farm.

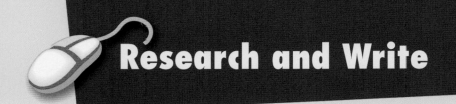

Research and Write

Write About Your Community

You read about one community in New York City. Now find out more about your own community. What was it like long ago? How has it changed? How has it stayed the same? What makes it special today?

Research
Collect books and reference materials, or go online.

Read and Take Notes
As you read, take notes and draw pictures.

Write
Write a postcard to a pen pal telling about your community. Talk about its history. Describe what the community looks like now and why people should come for a visit. Draw a picture of what you like best about your community.

Read and Compare

Read More About Communities

Find and read other books about communities. As you read, think about these questions.

- What is special about this community?
- How does this community meet people's needs?
- How is this community like or unlike other communities that I know?

Books to Read

▲ Learn about different types of communities and the people who live in them.

▲ See how this community is similar to and different from your community.

▲ Read about a suburban community of the past.

Glossary

apartment (page 8)
A group of rooms where people live
Some people live in buildings with many apartments.

community (page 4)
A place where people live, work, and have fun together
A city is a big community.

custom (page 18)
A habit or typical way of doing something
Italians brought their customs to Little Italy.

festival (page 21)
A big celebration
People in Little Italy hold festivals like the Feast
of San Gennaro.

goods (page 9)
Things that are made or grown and then sold
People buy goods from a market.

government (page 12)
A group of people who run a community
The government makes sure services run smoothly.

immigrant (page 18)
A person who leaves home to settle in a new country
Many Italian immigrants moved to Little Italy.

law (page 13)
A community rule
Laws help keep people safe.

provide (page 8)
To give or supply
Communities provide services such as mail delivery.

public transportation (page 11)
A way of moving large numbers of people from place to place
Many people use public transportation to get around.

service (page 10)
Something useful that one person does for another
Education is one service communities provide.

shelter (page 8)
Protection
Communities offer shelter.

Index